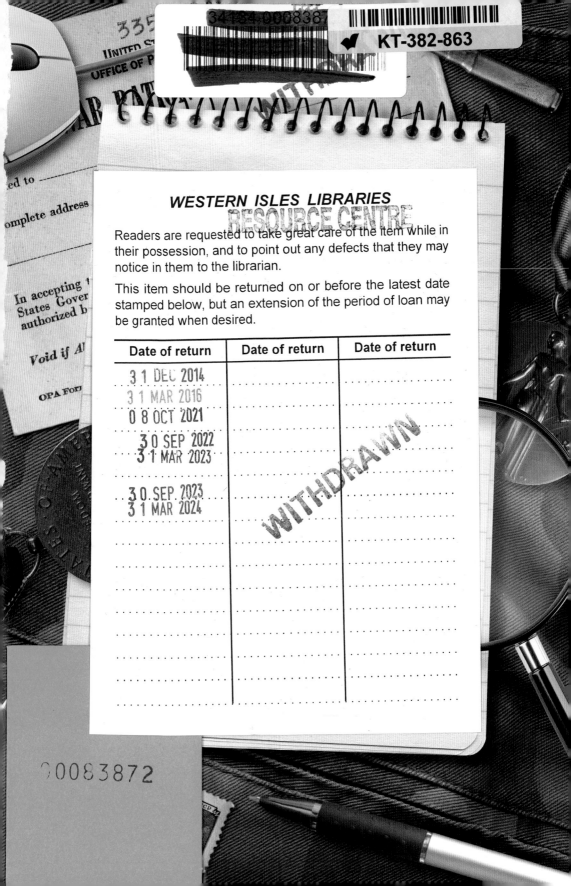

KT-382-863

## WESTERN ISLES LIBRARIES
RESOURCE CENTRE

Readers are requested to take great care of the item while in their possession, and to point out any defects that they may notice in them to the librarian.

This item should be returned on or before the latest date stamped below, but an extension of the period of loan may be granted when desired.

| Date of return | Date of return | Date of return |
|---|---|---|
| 3 1 DEC 2014 | | |
| 3 1 MAR 2016 | | |
| 0 8 OCT 2021 | | |
| 3 0 SEP 2022 | | |
| 3 1 MAR 2023 | | |
| 3 0 SEP 2023 | | |
| 3 1 MAR 2024 | | |

WITHDRAWN

00083872

**www.raintreepublishers.co.uk**
Visit our website to find out
more information about
Raintree books.

**To order:**
☎ Phone 0845 6044371
🖷 Fax +44 (0) 1865 312263
✉ Email myorders@raintreepublishers.co.uk

Customers from outside the UK please telephone +44 1865 312262

Raintree is an imprint of Capstone Global
Library Limited, a company incorporated
in England and Wales having its registered
office at 7 Pilgrim Street, London, EC4V 6LB
- Registered company number: 6695582.

Text © Capstone Global Library Limited 2010
First published in paperback in 2011
The moral rights of the proprietor have
been asserted.

All rights reserved. No part of this publication
may be reproduced in any form or by any
means (including photocopying or storing
it in any medium by electronic means and
whether or not transiently or incidentally to
some other use of this publication) without
the written permission of the copyright owner,
except in accordance with the provisions
of the Copyright, Designs and Patents Act
1988 or under the terms of a licence issued
by the Copyright Licensing Agency, Saffron
House, 6–10 Kirby Street, London EC1N
8TS (www.cla.co.uk). Applications for the
copyright owner's written permission should
be addressed to the publisher.

Edited by Andrew Farrow and
    Rebecca Vickers
Designed by Steven Mead
Picture research by Ruth Blair
Production by Victoria Fitzgerald
Originated by Capstone Global Library Ltd
Printed and bound in China by South China
Printing Company Ltd

ISBN 978 0 431116 20 4 (hardback)
14 13 12 11 10
10 9 8 7 6 5 4 3 2 1

ISBN 978 0 431116 27 3 (paperback)
14 13 12 11 10
10 9 8 7 6 5 4 3 2 1

**British Library Cataloguing in
Publication Data**
Langley, Andrew.
    World War II. -- (Research it!)
    1. World War, 1939-1945--Research--
Methodology--Juvenile literature.
    I. Title II. Series
    940.5'3'072-dc22

**Acknowledgements**
We would like to thank the following for
permission to reproduce photographs:
The Art Archive: pp. **41** (Culver Pictures),
**13 bottom**; Corbis: pp. **33**, **35** (Bettmann)
**6** (Fancy/Veer), **4**, **38** (Hulton-Deutsch
Collection); ©Imperial War Museum: p. **32**
(Laura Knight); istockphoto: p. **51** (©Pamela
Moore, Luther Zimmerman); Mary Evans
Picture Library: pp. **16** (Imagno), **20**, **26**;
Mirrorpix: p. **28** (Philip Zec); Rex Features:
pp. **13 top** (C.WisHisSoc/Everett), **31** (CSU
Archives/Everett Collection), **37** (Alinari),
**18**; ©shutterstock and ©iStockphoto:
design features.

The main cover image of the "Dig for Victory"
poster is reproduced with permission of
Bridgeman Art Library/©English School/
Stapleton Collection and the main cover
image of children having a gas mask drill
is reproduced with permission of Corbis/
©Bettmann. The background images are
reproduced with the permission of the
following: iStockphoto (©Janne Ahvo,
©Olena Druzhynina, ©Ray Roper, ©Luther
Zimmerman) and shutterstock (©Sascha
Burkard, ©Lars Lindblad, ©Picsfive).

We would like to thank Stewart Ross for his
invaluable help in the preparation of this
book.

Every effort has been made to contact
copyright holders of material reproduced in
this book. Any omissions will be rectified in
subsequent printings if notice is given to the
publisher.

All the Internet addresses (URLs) given in this
book were valid at the time of going to press.
However, due to the dynamic nature of the
Internet, some addresses may have changed,
or sites may have changed or ceased to
exist since publication. While the author and
publisher regret any inconvenience this may
cause readers, no responsibility for any such
changes can be accepted by either the author
or the publisher.

# Contents

Some words are printed in bold, **like this**. You can find out what they mean by looking in the glossary.

# Researching World War II

World War II (also known as the Second World War) was the biggest conflict in history. The fighting covered most of the globe, from Western Europe right round to the Pacific. Nearly all of the world's nations were caught up in it, directly or indirectly. Up to 70 million people died during the war, and 100 million served in the world's armies. The war also touched the lives of many millions more.

## Finding out about the war

Obviously World War II is a gigantic subject. So how do you begin finding out about it? Perhaps you want to research a topic for a school report, or for homework, coursework, or some other assignment. To get a full and balanced picture of your topic, you need to do research. There is a huge variety of methods and sources for your research, and they can sometimes seem confusing and daunting.

This book is a guide to researching World War II. You will find suggestions for possible research questions, and the basic tools needed to answer them. The book provides information about key themes, questions, and issues. There is advice on how to find, evaluate, and present information, and how to make use of graphic organizers and other aids.

*Very few people were unaffected by World War II. Throughout Europe, huge numbers of civilians lost their homes and possessions.*

## What is evidence?

First of all, what are you looking for in your research? The answer is: evidence. This is the raw material which gives a firm base for your project. Without facts and other hard evidence you will not be able to build up a truthful and rounded picture of the topic, or back up your conclusions.

Historians usually divide their sources of evidence into two kinds – primary and secondary. **Primary sources** come from the time of the event, or from people who were there. They are usually created by people who were there and can describe the scene directly. **Secondary sources** are usually created later. They are new records or interpretations of events, using primary or other secondary source material.

## Where do you find evidence?

There are many places to look for sources of information about World War II. A library is the obvious starting point. Here you can find books of all kinds, including autobiographies, diaries, and collections of letters, as well as modern studies by historians. Many libraries can also give you access to DVDs, maps, newspaper **archives**, and other useful material.

The Internet offers a vast choice of World War II sites – some very helpful, but many not. Then there are photographs, **newsreel** films, and sound recordings. Museums such as the Imperial War Museum in London have large collections of World War II objects, such as uniforms and weapons. You can also learn a lot by using your eyes and ears. Can you spot signs that your local town suffered bomb damage? Have you spoken with anyone who lived through the war?

### Primary and secondary sources

| Primary | Secondary |
|---|---|
| Diaries | History textbooks |
| Letters | Biographies |
| Photographs | Films of historical events |
| News film | Encyclopedias |
| Sound recordings | TV documentaries |
| Newspaper stories | |
| Eyewitness accounts | |
| Military reports | |

# Finding Your Way Around

## Planning and using research

Libraries, museums, and even the Internet can be confusing places. So get to know the best way to make use of them. Ask librarians and attendants for advice and directions to help you find the information you're after. For example, they can show you the indexes and databases available in the library. That's what they are there for. Ask friends, teachers, or parents about how to navigate Internet websites.

Learn to use the tools on offer. For example, textbooks and other reference works have a lot of built-in features to make life easier for the researcher. Do you know what a glossary is? How do you use an index? What can you learn from the contents list? Once you get accustomed to these features, your evidence gathering will become faster and simpler.

Soon the evidence will be piling up. If you are not careful, you can be swamped by facts, figures, references, quotations, and images. It is vital that you learn to organize your material right from the beginning, so you can keep track of every item. Good organization also encourages you to stay firmly focused on your chosen topic.

*With a laptop, a student can access the Internet from almost anywhere.*

There are tools to help here, too. Graphic organizers come in all shapes and sizes, and include charts, diagrams, webs, and tables. These will give structure to your project, helping you to plan the questions you want to answer and to lay out the results of your research.

## Think for yourself!

Research can take you into all sorts of interesting places. You'll find sources you never knew about. But are they telling the truth? Can you trust the evidence? Many writers are trying to convince you that their version of events is the right one. It is sometimes difficult to keep a balanced view of your topic.

Here are some questions to ask yourself about every piece of evidence you see:
- Is it fact or opinion?
- Does it come from a reliable source?
- Have you compared different accounts or statistics to get an all-round view?
- Are you thinking objectively – or are you just trying to prove a point?

## Organizing the facts

Here's a very simple kind of graphic organizer, called a source chart. It has three columns – one for recording a useful fact or quotation, the second for the book or site where you found it, and the third for the page or reference number:

**Name:** *A. Student*     **Topic:** *The Blitzkrieg*

| INFORMATION | SOURCE | PAGE |
|---|---|---|
| *How Germans developed "lightning war" tactics* | *BBC History website* | – |
| *German tanks break through at Sedan, France, May 1940* | *Chronicle of the Second World War, ed. Derrick Mercer (Longman, 1990)* | *85* |
| *Eyewitness account by British soldier of being wounded and taken prisoner in France* | *Witness to War, ed. Richard Aldrich (Doubleday, 2004)* | *115* |

# Step 1: An Overview

It's time to choose and research your topic. But it is crucial to start with a broad picture of World War II and its main events. Here are some of the most important questions about the causes and the course of the war. Answering these questions will help you to build a framework round your own special project and put it into context.

## Using the 5 Ws

Here is an example of how you can use the five Ws in your World War II research:

**1. What?** A brief definition.
*World War II was a global military conflict which lasted from 1939 to 1945 and involved most nations of the world. It killed more people and covered a much larger area than any other war in history.*

**2. Why?** The main causes of the war.

<u>Defeat and debt</u>
*The **Treaty** that ended World War I placed huge penalties on a defeated Germany. As well as losing huge areas of territory, the Germans had to pay crippling sums of money to the victors. This caused great resentment in Germany.*

### The 5 Ws

Every topic – big or small – can be approached in the same way. Ask yourself five simple questions about it:
What? Why? Where? When? Who?

These are the 5 Ws. You can ask and answer them in any order. Once this is done, you will have a basic outline of the subject. Just as important, you will also have a structure that allows you to evaluate the information you find when you begin your research. Always ask yourself this question: Does this piece of evidence help to answer any of the 5 Ws?

<u>The Great Depression</u>
*A world economic crisis during the early 1930s brought poverty and mass unemployment to much of Europe and the USA. This **depression** caused unrest and weakened the power of many **democratic** governments.*

<u>The rise of the dictators</u>
***Dictators** took power in several countries during the 1920s and 1930s and crushed any opposition. Germany, Japan, Italy, and the **Soviet Union** (USSR) were all dictatorships.*

*Expansionism*

*Germany, Italy, and Japan invaded neighbouring countries. They wanted to build empires and seize valuable resources. This is known as **expansionism**. The Nazi leaders of Germany also wanted revenge for the defeat in 1918, and the destruction of races and peoples they considered "inferior" (such as the Slavs and the Jews). Many European leaders wanted desperately to prevent another world war. So, they allowed Hitler to seize territory, hoping that he would soon be satisfied and stop. This non-aggressive policy was known as **appeasement**.*

3. **Where?** The main areas where the war was fought. This question can be best answered using graphics instead of words – such as maps showing the major **theatres of war**. Maps are a vital part of research for a huge and complicated subject like World War II. As well as providing evidence, they help you to understand the geographical context of your topic. In your notes, you can add simple sketch maps based on the maps you find. Here are possible sources of suitable maps:

   - a world atlas (very accurate and detailed, but no information about historical events)
   - the Internet (a huge range but not always reliable or detailed enough)
   - history books (very reliable, but maps usually relate to specific battles or events)
   - a historical atlas (a good historical atlas should be accurate, detailed, and wide-ranging)

This map shows the main theatres of war in July 1940.

4.  **When?** Dates are important in any study of history. One of the best
    ways of presenting dates is in a timeline. This can help you conduct your
    research and present facts in your report. A timeline can be a simple
    chart of just a few important dates or can be presented in a more graphic
    way, with dates spread across or down the page. A fuller, more complete
    timeline can include main events and dates of the build-up to war, as well
    as the conflict itself:

## World War II Timeline

| | | |
|---|---|---|
| **1933** | January 30 | Hitler is elected Chancellor of Germany |
| **1934** | August | Hitler becomes Führer (dictator) of Germany |
| **1935** | March | Hitler begins to build up German armed forces |
| | September | New laws in Germany take away the rights of Jews |
| **1936** | March | German troops occupy the Rhineland |
| | May | Italy conquers Abyssinia (modern Ethiopia) |
| **1938** | March 13 | Germany forms a union ("*Anschluss*") with Austria |
| | October | German troops march into the Sudetenland region of Czechoslovakia |
| **1939** | March 15 | Germany begins invasion of Czechoslovakia |
| | August 23 | Germany and the Soviet Union sign a non-aggression pact |
| | September 1 | Germany invades Poland |
| | September 3 | Britain and France (the Allies) declare war on Germany: World War II begins |
| **1940** | April 9 | Germany begins invasion of Denmark and Norway |
| | May 10 | German **blitzkrieg** invasion of the Netherlands starts, to be followed by invasions of Belgium and France; Winston Churchill becomes head of the British government |
| | June 10 | Italy joins the war on Germany's side (the Axis) |
| | June 14 | Paris, the French capital, falls to the Germans |
| | June 22 | France signs an armistice with Germany |
| | July–October | Battle of Britain – German bombing raids on British cities (including the London Blitz) |

| 1941 | April | Axis troops begin invasions of Yugoslavia and Greece |
|------|-------|-----|
| | June 22 | German troops invade Soviet Union: the Soviets join the side of the Allies |
| | December 7 | Japanese aircraft attack the U.S. naval fleet at Pearl Harbor, Hawaii |
| | December 8 | Britain and the USA declare war on Japan |
| 1942 | February 15 | Japanese capture Singapore from the British |
| | June 6 | U.S. navy defeats Japanese forces in the Battle of Midway (Pacific) |
| | November 6 | Allied forces defeat Axis armies at El Alamein, North Africa |
| 1943 | November | The Soviet Union defeats the Germans at the Battle of Stalingrad |
| | May 13 | Axis forces in North Africa surrender |
| | July 10 | Allied troops invade Italy from the south |
| | September 8 | Italy surrenders to Allies |
| 1944 | January | Soviet army drives besieging Germans from Leningrad |
| | June 6 | **D-Day** – Allies launch a massive invasion in Normandy, France |
| | August 25 | Paris is **liberated** from the Germans |
| | October | Allied troops recapture the Philippines from the Japanese |
| 1945 | March | U.S. troops capture Iwo Jima; Allies cross the River Rhine into Germany |
| | April 22 | Soviet troops enter Berlin |
| | April 30 | Hitler commits suicide |
| | May 8 | German forces surrender throughout Europe: the Allies celebrate VE (Victory in Europe) Day |
| | August 6 & 9 | U.S. aircraft drop **atomic bombs** on Japanese cities of Hiroshima and Nagasaki |
| | August 14 | Japan surrenders |
| | August 15 | Allies celebrate VJ (Victory over Japan) Day; war ends. |

**5. Who?** The main nations on the opposing sides and their political leaders.
_The Allies_
_United Kingdom and its Empire: Winston S. Churchill_
_USA: Franklin D. Roosevelt, then Harry S Truman_
_Soviet Union: Joseph Stalin_
_(Other Allied powers include France, Australia, Canada, New Zealand,_
_Greece, Yugoslavia, Denmark, and India)_

_The Axis_
_Germany: Adolf Hitler_
_Japan: Hideki Tojo_
_Italy: Benito Mussolini_
_(Other Axis powers include Hungary, Bulgaria, Albania, and Romania)_

Altogether, about 60 countries took part in the war. The remainder (including Switzerland, Spain, and Ireland) stayed **neutral**.

## Identifying the major themes

World War II covered vast areas of the world and involved millions of people. The range of battles, personalities, triumphs, disasters, and tragedies was huge and can be bewildering for a researcher. So it is sensible to concentrate on just a few of the most important events and themes from the conflict. Here is a selection. You may be able to add some more of your own.

### Blitzkrieg

The war opened with rapid German invasions of Northern Europe and France. Their new method of blitzkrieg ("lightning war") used speed and surprise to smash through enemy resistance. Tanks drove deep into each country, while bombers destroyed communications systems. After them the infantry established firm control.

### The Holocaust

Hitler soon developed plans for a **"Final Solution"** – to murder all European Jews. Jewish men, women, and children in conquered states were rounded up and sent to **concentration camps**, where most were shot or gassed. Many others died from disease or torture. Over 6 million Jews perished during the war. This is now know as the Holocaust.

### The home front

Civilians in many lands suffered the horrors of warfare. Millions of **refugees** were forced to flee their homes to escape the carnage. Even those far from the front line were affected – by bombing raids, food rationing, and mass evacuation. The war also forced social change, including a huge increase in the employment of women.

## The USA joins the war

The United States had been neutral since the outbreak of war, despite sympathizing with the Allies. In December 1941, Japanese aircraft attacked the U.S. Pacific fleet in Hawaii without warning, drawing the United States into the war. The added weight of the U.S. armed forces changed the balance of the conflict and made an Allied victory certain.

*The Japanese attack on Pearl Harbor caused the USA to declare war on the Axis powers and Japan.*

*These German soldiers are using an Enigma code machine.*

## The secret war

The work of spies and **code breakers** had a crucial impact on the war. The most important achievement was the Allied cracking of the German **cipher** called **Enigma**. This allowed them to have advance warning of Axis attacks in many areas, and led to several vital battlefield successes.

## The atomic bomb

In August 1945, the Americans dropped the first atomic bomb on the Japanese city of Hiroshima, killing more than 100,000 people. This, and the bombing of Nagasaki three days later, shocked Japan into surrendering. The need for a full-scale invasion was avoided. The awesome power of **nuclear** weapons was to haunt the world ever afterwards.

# Step 2: The Basics

We have looked at some of the main aspects of World War II. We've seen that a huge subject like this can be broken down into separate elements: the causes, the events, the major issues, the personalities, and the results. The next step in the process is to find out more about the tools of research, and how they can be used to determine what we're looking for and how we find it.

## Locating the basic facts

Where would you look for a straightforward outline of World War II facts? The two most obvious sources, easily available to most people, are the Internet and books. But both of them have minus points as well as plus points.

### The Internet

Access to the World Wide Web is easy – in schools, colleges, libraries, homes, and many other places. It is also (as the name says) available all over the world. So, you have access to the same information wherever you are. This comes in every form imaginable, from **blogs** and discussion forums to news archives and film clips.

A big and fairly recent event like World War II is thoroughly covered on the Internet. And, because it concerned so many countries, you can find sites relating to every theatre of the conflict, and every nation that took part, no matter how small. For instance, you can find out about the major role played by the Native American Navajo people. Navajo radio operators were used by U.S. forces to transmit secret messages in the Navajo language, which the Germans could not understand or translate. (Look under "Navajo Code Talkers".)

*Internet pluses*: At the click of a mouse, there is a huge variety of sites to choose from. They cover every educational level, ranging from primary school to university and beyond. You can access them fast, and refine your research online to make more accurate requests. Online subscription sites and sites provided by important museums and other public bodies are the most reliable.

*Internet minuses*: There's too much choice. Enter "World War II" into a search engine and you'll be faced with over 50 million sites, all something to do with the subject. Most of these will be useless, and include advertisements, ignorant blogs, and chatrooms. It's easy to waste a lot of time trawling through them.

## The four important rules to remember when using the Internet

1. *Be precise with your search.* The more specific you can be with your demands, the quicker you'll find the information you want. Usually, this will mean narrowing your topic down. If you enter just "Battle Britain", for example, you'll get all the sites that include the words "Battle" and "Britain". Instead, enter something more detailed, such as "Battle Britain August 1940", or "Battle Britain RAF Fighter Command".

2. *Check the date of the website.* Some information, even about World War II, can become out-of-date very quickly, as fresh research finds new facts and perspectives. For instance, there are no completely reliable statistics about the number of casualties (military or civilian) during the conflict. New evidence is still being found which means the figures have to be altered.

3. *Check the source of the website.* Ask yourself: what kind of authority does this writer have? Anybody can set up their own site and fill it with their own views and their own version of events. The result can be enlightening and intelligent – or it can be malicious, unbalanced, and plain wrong. Always look to see who produced the site, and where they are coming from. Use your own judgement about their intentions.

4. *Keep concentrating.* The Internet is buzzing with bright and attractive sites and links aimed at grabbing your attention. It's very easy to be distracted by them, and forget what you were looking for at the outset. So stay focused on your topic, and on the original reason for your research.

## Books

The reference and history sections in a library will have all sorts of books that provide the basic facts about World War II. You are unlikely to find exactly the same selection of books in every library, because each one has a different stock (collection of titles). However, almost any book is available. If you can't see what you want, simply look in the library's online catalogue and order it.

Many reference books share the useful common elements listed below.

- Contents: At the beginning of the book is a table of the contents. This is a list of the chapter titles and other sections contained in the book, with the number of the page they start on.
- Glossary: The book may contain difficult words or obscure technical terms. These are listed in alphabetical order with definitions in the glossary.
- Bibliography: The bibliography is an alphabetical list of the other books that the author referred to when writing. Each book's author, publisher, and publication date is given.
- Index: At the end of the book is the Index, the most useful tool of all. It is an alphabetical list of names, terms, and subjects found in the text. Next to each entry is a list of the page numbers containing the references.

*This picture taken at the time shows Polish Jews being rounded up by German soldiers in Warsaw.*

*Book pluses*: Books are portable and simple to handle. Most will have indexes, which makes life easy when you're looking for specific references. Also, books are likely to be pretty accurate and serious in their aims (unlike a lot of websites), because publishers have to get things right or go out of business.

*Book minuses*: There's often too little choice. Most libraries and bookshops only have a small selection of books on a particular subject (even World War II), so you may have to order what you want and then wait days till they arrive. Some history books can look daunting. But they usually have the special features listed above that help you to find what you want. Learn to use these, and your research work will be quicker and more efficient.

## What kinds of reference book are good for research?

1. *Encyclopedias* Some encyclopedias come in a single large volume, while others fill whole shelves with twenty or more volumes. The entries are arranged in alphabetical or theme order and are usually straightforward to find. In general, the bigger the encyclopedia, the more detailed information it will contain.

2. *Dictionaries* A dictionary is usually devoted to a single subject. There are, for example, dictionaries about World War II, about the history of warfare, about major battles, and about specific topics, such as the Holocaust. The entries are again alphabetical and easy to locate.

3. *Chronologies* A **chronology** is another word for a timeline. Brief descriptions of events are laid out in date order, sometimes with features on major topics. Chronologies are ideal for getting an understanding of the shape of the war, and how a lot of things were happening at the same time.

4. *Concise accounts* There are several short histories of World War II which provide the basic facts in a quickly readable form. They will give you an overall "feel" for the conflict in more detail than an encyclopedia or a chronology.

## Graphic organizers

Graphic organizers are tools to help you to arrange and keep a record of your research. They are a pictorial way of organizing information in an easy and instantly understandable form. An organizer usually consists of a one-page form, with blank areas for the student to enter facts, quotations, ideas, and arguments. You will find examples of the main graphic organizers as you read through this book.

Using graphic organizers can be vital in helping you keep track of your sources. With hundreds of websites to look at and piles of books to trawl through, you won't be short of research material. But the volume of information can quickly grow into a mountain. As you work, note down the exact source of each fact or opinion or quotation using a graphic organizer, such as a source chart (see page 7). This can help you keep track of what came from where or who said what. Noting sources is a vital part of research. This is partly because it allows you to find a source again easily. But it is also vital because many teachers insist that students give two separate sources for each major fact. So, the sources have to agree. This is called confirming a fact. But what happens if you cannot find a second source to confirm a piece of evidence? The fact may be true, but has to remain unconfirmed. You must state this in your writing or presentation.

*During the London Blitz, bombs and shells destroyed whole areas of the city. Not everyone had access to shelters at home. The KWL chart on page 19 will help you focus on questions relating to life during the London Blitz.*

There are all sorts of graphic organizers with strange names, such as fishbone maps, Venn diagrams (see page 45), flow charts, and concept webs (see page 23). Some are simply for setting out research findings so they are easy to access and clear to read. Some are models that help you solve problems by posing a question, offering possible solutions, and reaching a conclusion. Other graphic organizers are designed for presenting your work to others and illustrating specific points in a form which is dramatic and easy to understand.

## A KWL chart

KWL is a simple and effective kind of graphic organizer. It has three columns, headed:

What I **K**now          What I **W**ant to Know          What I **L**earned

Fill in the first two columns (**K** and **W**) before you start your research, and the third column (**L**) as you work. This encourages you to keep track of your knowledge, to plan ahead, and to stay focused in your research.

Here is a filled in example on the topic of the home front, posing the question:
*What was it like to live through the London Blitz?*

| What I **K**now | What I **W**ant to Know | What I **L**earned |
|---|---|---|
| *Families slept in bomb shelters.* | *What was it like inside an **Anderson shelter**?* | *Cramped, cold, dark, and damp. Moisture dripped off the curved steel ceiling.* |
| *Not everybody had a shelter at home.* | *Where else could people hide from bombing raids?* | *Many Londoners slept on underground platforms and in the basements of big stores.* |
| *More than 2 million Londoners lost their homes in the Blitz.* | *Where did homeless people go?* | *Rest centres were set up in public buildings. Many bombed-out Londoners stayed with neighbours or relatives.* |

# Step 3: Digging Deeper

So far, this book has looked at the background facts about World War II, and introduced you to the basic tools needed to begin research. Now it is time to zoom in on your special topic.

## How to select a topic

Of course, you may have no choice. Some subjects are required to be studied in specific ways, or your teacher may guide you into a certain area. On the other hand, you may be free to choose your own topic for research within the larger subject area. Is there an aspect of World War II which especially interests you? If not, try reading more deeply into the background of the conflict to stimulate your interest.

Here are some suggestions for topics to research. You could study:

- The causes of the war (aggression, economic depression, the rise of **fascism**, appeasement)
- A major turning point (the Battle of Britain, Hitler's invasion of Russia, the entry of the USA into the conflict, D-Day)
- A leader who made a crucial impact (political leaders – Hitler, Churchill, Hirohito, Stalin, Roosevelt; or military ones – Eisenhower, Patton, Montgomery, Rommel)

*Adolf Hitler is shown here on stage addressing a Nazi meeting in Germany under the sign of the swastika.*

- The **totalitarian** nations in the war (Germany, Japan, Italy, the Soviet Union. In what ways were they similar or dissimilar?)
- The Nazi policy of purifying their race (what led to the "Final Solution" and the Holocaust?)
- A technological or other advance developed in wartime (the atomic bomb, **radar**, rockets, computers)
- A major social or political effect of the war (the changed role of women, the **Iron Curtain**, the creation of Israel).

## Narrowing down your topic

Always concentrate on finding the most convenient and least complicated path to your evidence. You may have chosen (or been assigned) a very broad topic to research, such as "The War in the Pacific" or "The Rise of Fascism". These are such big subjects that you might be overwhelmed by the weight of information you find. The answer might be to narrow the topic down. This will make your job of researching and writing much easier. You need to find key words related to your topic which will enable you to focus on a smaller research area. You may find these in a book's index or in an online library catalogue, which will show topics related to your subject.

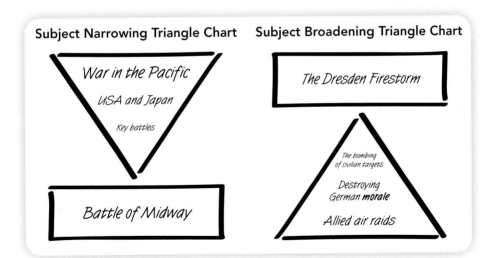

**Subject Narrowing Triangle Chart**

*War in the Pacific*

*USA and Japan*

*Key battles*

*Battle of Midway*

**Subject Broadening Triangle Chart**

*The Dresden Firestorm*

*The bombing of civilian targets*

*Destroying German **morale***

*Allied air raids*

## Broadening it out

Your topic may be a very narrow one to research, such as "The Dresden **Firestorm**". This can cause problems because there may not be enough specific information on it. You may also have difficulty in putting the subject in context. In this case, you can go the other way and broaden the topic, again using an index or catalogue.

335488

UNITED STATES OF
~CE OF PRICE AD~

## Getting started

You may already know quite a bit about your topic. Or you may know next to nothing. Either way, you can start the research project in the same manner. First, get to know the outlines of the topic by looking in encyclopedias and general websites (as we have already seen). Write down a list of the four or five basic elements. Now the real research work can begin.

Ask yourself: what do I need to discover next? Decide on your lines of inquiry. Write a question or a research aim next to each entry on the list. This gives you an overall framework for your project. Questions will guide you and spur you on to discover more evidence over a wider area.

### Using a concept web

At this stage, you may need another kind of graphic organizer to record your research findings in a clear manner. A concept web is ideal for this. At the centre of the web (like a spider) is a bubble containing one of your questions. Lines radiate out from it, each with a box containing a different aspect of the question. And more lines branch out from these, with supporting facts or details. In this way, you can set down a question and its answers in an easily accessible way on a single page.

## Tips for taking notes

The main work of research is not just finding the sources – it is recording the evidence you find. Once again, this needs to be done as efficiently as possible. You don't want to end up with a mountain of dull, featureless pages. Here are a few tips to help you:

- Be selective. Don't just copy down everything you read. Pick out the most important and relevant facts to record in your own words.
- Break up your notes into sections or paragraphs, one for each strand of the topic, with a gap between them.
- Think up a brief but punchy heading for each section. Write it in bold or underlined script.
- Break up each section or paragraph as far as possible into lists: number each item.
- Insert key dates in the left hand margin. These will give a firm framework to your notes.
- Have a consistent style. Decide on a format and stick to it. This makes note-taking speedier.

For example, if the topic is The Holocaust, one of the questions could be: *How did the Nazi persecution of Jews begin?* This is how a concept web might look:

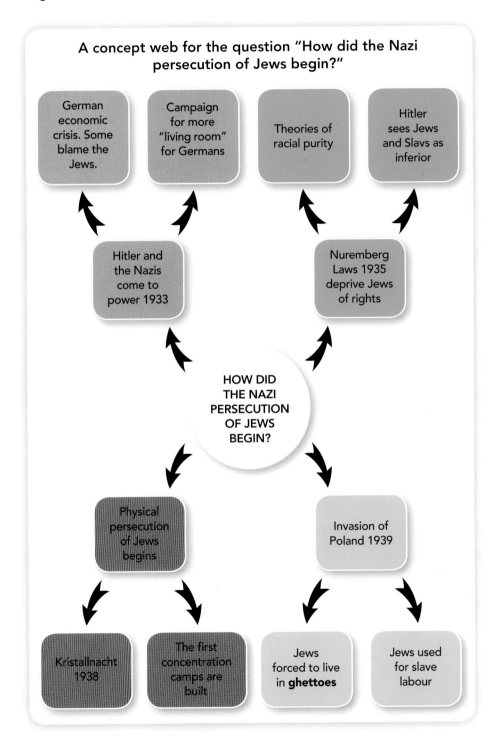

**A concept web for the question "How did the Nazi persecution of Jews begin?"**

German economic crisis. Some blame the Jews.

Campaign for more "living room" for Germans

Theories of racial purity

Hitler sees Jews and Slavs as inferior

Hitler and the Nazis come to power 1933

Nuremberg Laws 1935 deprive Jews of rights

**HOW DID THE NAZI PERSECUTION OF JEWS BEGIN?**

Physical persecution of Jews begins

Invasion of Poland 1939

Kristallnacht 1938

The first concentration camps are built

Jews forced to live in **ghettoes**

Jews used for slave labour

# Plagiarism

**Plagiarism** means cheating by stealing the writings or thoughts of other people. If you submit someone else's words and ideas and call them your own, then you are plagiarizing. It's easy to do this by accident. You can copy down a sentence from a book or website, forget where you found it, but still include it in your presentation. The Internet makes plagiarism much easier. Whole passages can be cut from an online source and pasted into research notes. But there are now many ways (including special computer software) in which this can be spotted, and the original site can soon be found. A good teacher or assessor will also become suspicious if a piece of work is written differently from a student's normal style.

So take steps to avoid any chance of plagiarizing. Make a careful note of anything you record for your research – for example, who wrote it and what page of the book it was on. Always put quotation marks around any passage you copy directly. And, always give credit to the author of quoted material, either in the text or in a footnote. Always trust your own ability to present information in your own way. It will give you great satisfaction and increase your confidence.

## Think critically about your sources

In your research, you'll have contact with many different kinds of source – on paper, on screen, and maybe even in person. Can you trust them all? How do you decide which sources are reliable, and which are not? Learn to think critically about what you read. This checklist suggests some factors to bear in mind:

- There is a difference between fact and opinion: learn to tell one from another.
- There are several ways of looking at any issue: identify the main points where sources agree – or disagree.
- All writers or chroniclers have their own agendas and their own special points to make: be on the look out for dishonesty and bias.
- You can only use the evidence that is available: evaluate it fairly and completely.

## Skimming and scanning

Obviously there's no time to read every single word of a book or a website when you are researching a topic. What is more, there's no need – you are only looking for information about a specific subject. So, speed up your reading with two simple techniques.

The first is called *skimming*. When faced with a large amount of text, look quickly through the contents list, titles, subheadings, captions, and maybe first and last sentences. Look out for any references which could be relevant to your research. Skimming will show whether it's worth reading in more detail. Next comes *scanning*, which is useful for finding more specific information. Run your eye down the page, reading selectively and skipping through the text. Pick out key words or phrases and note their location.

## Evidence can be out of date

History does not stand still. Obviously, the basic facts about World War II are well established, but many aspects are changing all the time. New evidence comes to light, mistakes are corrected, and events are interpreted in different ways by a new generation. As a result, some sources (even books) will become misleading or factually incorrect over the years. This makes double-checking even more important. For example, the work of the Allied code breakers at Bletchley Park in Britain was kept almost entirely secret for many years after the war. Historians had no access to information about the cracking of the German Enigma cipher. Therefore, they did not know about the crucial effect this had on many major events, including the Battle of Britain and the Normandy landings. The full details of the Enigma story were only released in the 1970s, after which many accounts of the war had to be revised.

## Using SQ3R

SQ3R is an aid to reading and retaining information efficiently. The name comes from the five steps of the strategy: **S**urvey, **Q**uestion, and the **3 Rs** (**R**ead, **R**ecall, **R**eview).

**S** **S**urvey: First, skim through the entire passage or site. Take note of any headings and summaries you see. Don't read in detail at this point, but try to jot down up to six major ideas in the passage.

**Q** **Q**uestion: Write down a list of questions to ask yourself. What is this passage about? What questions is it trying to answer? Does it answer any of your own queries? Repeat this process with each paragraph or section.

**R** **R**ead: Carefully read through each section, looking for answers to your questions. (If the passage is on a website, you may find it easier to print it out first.)

**R** **R**ecall: Make key phrases, in your own words, to summarize each of the major points. Write them down or speak them out loud.

**R** **R**eview: You should end up with a list of key phrases and answers to questions. Read through them again to make sure you've covered everything. See if you can remember them without looking at the list. If you can't remember one of these key points, you need to reread the section it refers to.

# Step 4: Documents

Documents are the raw material of history. They are the primary sources, usually written at the time by people who were directly involved with events, such as soldiers, refugees, politicians, and eyewitnesses of all kinds. Documents come in many forms, from diaries and letters to poems and newspaper reports. World War II has left a very rich legacy of such sources.

## How it looked at the time

The diaries and **memoirs** of famous Allied leaders, such as Winston Churchill, Harry S Truman, and Charles de Gaulle and of military commanders, such as Field Marshal Montgomery and General (later, President) Eisenhower, have all been published in book form. But there are not many personal stories of Axis leaders, because most died in or just after the war and left no records. One of the few accounts from inside the Nazi **Third Reich** is by Albert Speer, one of Hitler's top ministers.

Many more first-hand accounts were written by ordinary people – soldiers, seamen, prisoners of war, housewives, farmers, aid workers, and doctors. The most famous war diary of all was written by Anne Frank, a schoolgirl in hiding in Nazi-occupied Amsterdam. However, many of these journals and memoirs are hard to obtain, and most have never been published at all.

### Official records

Details of the conflict and the people who fought in it are also contained in official archives. Each government kept a record of the soldiers, sailors, and air crew

*This photo shows a page from the famous diary of Anne Frank.*

who entered the armed forces, where they went, and how long they served. Commanders in the field compiled reports of troop movements, battles, and other military events. Organizations like the Red Cross monitored the huge numbers of prisoners of war on both sides.

There are many other kinds of public records that might have useful information. Government documents from the war years tell us what happened in parliaments and ministries. Registers of births, marriages, and deaths give the bare outlines of a person's life. Then there are local histories and family histories, all of which can contain helpful material. Researching family history can be a very rewarding activity – and can be easily done.

### Getting access

Where can we find documents? The most popular ones, such as Anne Frank's diary or Winston Churchill's account of the war, can easily be found in libraries and bookshops. But the majority of them, unfortunately, are available in limited forms. Often the only way to read them is in printed collections of extracts. Ask your local librarian for help in locating these items.

There is online access to many official documents, including army enlistment registers and lists of combatants who received medals. Once again, it is vital to refine your search aims so you find the facts you're after quickly and efficiently.

Best of all, pay a visit to your local public records office or the national archives (check their website first). There are also several organizations which hold vast collections of personal and public war documents, such as the Imperial War Museum in London.

## War poetry

Can poetry be used as research material? Poems can sometimes convey the emotional experience of fighting in a war and killing people better than prose accounts in diaries or letters. Here is a description of the moment a soldier shoots one of the enemy:

Now in my dial of glass appears
the soldier who is going to die.
He smiles, and moves about in ways
his mother knows, habits of his.
The wires touch his face: I cry
Now. Death, like a familiar, hears

and look, has made a man of dust
of a man of flesh. This sorcery
I do. Being damned, I am amused
to see the centre of love diffused
and the waves of love travel into vacancy.
How easy it is to make a ghost.

From the poem "How to Kill" by Keith Douglas, who died in World War II during the 1944 Normandy invasion (in Keith Douglas: The Complete Poems. London: Faber, 2000.).

# Newspapers

One of the most useful primary sources for World War II research are newspapers. They contain vast amounts of raw material – reports from the front line of the conflict, government announcements, the text of important speeches, and news of the home front. They also convey the mood of the time in which they were written. But newspapers should be used with caution. They were often produced at speed, and influenced by government or other **propaganda**. The facts are not always reliable.

National newspapers covered the main events of the war. Many of them had reporters who moved with the troops and described events as they happened (such as the D-Day landings). Local newspapers concentrated on local news and views. This makes them an important source of evidence about how ordinary people coped with the dangers and difficulties of wartime life, including rationing, being an evacuee, and bombing raids.

## How to access and read old newspapers

Newspapers are easy to access. Many major papers have their archives available online, which means that you can look at news as it was reported on a specific day or month during the war. Most of these archives include an index, which enables you to be precise in your research.

Some local and national newspapers are also available in **microfiche** form, which you can view at your library. A newspaper is made up of several different elements. Which do you think will be most useful in research?

"Here you are! Don't lose it again!"

*One of the great lasting images from World War II is Zec's cartoon of an Allied soldier handing over the symbol of victory and peace in Europe to the world.*

- *Headlines* Good for making a quick point, but short on detail: use as hard-hitting illustrations.
- *News reports* Detailed stories of latest developments in the war, both at home and in the various theatres around the world: often very good first-hand accounts.
- *Comment pieces* Articles on the course of the war by leading writers and politicians: very useful for opinions and informed views.
- *Feature articles* Everything from music and sport to gardening and cooking: a valuable source of information about **morale** and popular culture in this period.
- *Photographs and maps* Clear evidence and diagrams of how the war was being fought.
- *Cartoons* The best cartoons, such as those by David Low and Philip Zec, created lasting images which summed up crucial moments or attitudes.

## Propaganda

"Propaganda" means using publicity to put across a message or idea. During World War II, a huge amount of propaganda was produced by governments on both sides. It had two main aims: to make people angry and united against the enemy, and to urge them to act in their country's interest (for instance, by working hard, looking out for spies, or not wasting resources). You can find many examples of propaganda in books, websites, and museums. But remember to treat them critically: after all, they were not meant to be truthful or unbiased.

- Newspapers, of course, were the perfect way of spreading government propaganda. Papers were cheap, and nearly everybody bought one every day.
- Leaflets were dropped in their millions over enemy or occupied territory. They made threats, or encouraged people to surrender.
- Radio broadcasts were a new form of propaganda, intended to affect morale. The most famous were made from Germany by "Lord Haw-Haw" (William Joyce) and from Japan by "Tokyo Rose".
- Posters were pasted on walls and boards and in public transport. The best were hard-hitting and direct. Many have been preserved as classic works of propaganda – and art.

## Eyewitness accounts: Are they reliable?

First-hand descriptions of war are some of the most exciting (and shocking) of all primary sources. The memories of a concentration camp survivor, or an agent behind enemy lines, or a victim of Russian brutality in Berlin can give us vivid impressions of the worst horrors of the conflict. Even the less dramatic experiences can help build a realistic picture of ordinary life in wartime.

All the same, a researcher has to think critically about these records. Various things can colour the accounts. The writers may be in a hurry or be wounded, angry, or frightened. They may be writing long after the event, and make up what they cannot remember exactly. They may alter things to make their own actions look better. If possible, get evidence about a specific event from more than one primary source. This may help to confirm how things happened. And, even if the accounts disagree with each other, they will help to produce a much broader picture.

### How they saw it: The atom bomb hits Hiroshima

Early on the morning of 6 August 1945, a U.S. aircraft dropped the first–ever nuclear weapon on the Japanese city of Hiroshima. This was how the awful event was seen, by those on the bomber, from Hiroshima itself, and from far away in the USA:

**The view from above**
*"A bright light filled the plane. We turned to look back at Hiroshima. The city was hidden by that awful cloud boiling up, mushrooming, terrible, and incredibly tall."*
(Paul Tibbets, pilot)

*"Where we had seen a clear city two minutes before, we could now no longer see the city. We could see smoke and fires creeping up the sides of the mountains."*
(Robert Lewis, co-pilot)

*"The mushroom itself was a spectacular sight, a bubbling mass of purple–gray smoke and you could see it had a red core in it and everything was burning inside."*
(Robert Caron, tail gunner)

**The view from below**
*"I saw that Hiroshima had been completely levelled to the ground, and my heart shook like a great wave."*
(Yoko Ota, writer)

*This photo shows the flattened ruins of the Japanese city of Hiroshima after the atomic blast that shocked the world.*

*"Black smoke was billowing up and we could hear the sound of big things exploding. There was a strange smell all over. Blue-green balls of fire were drifting around."*
(Anon, five-year-old girl)

*"People came fleeing from the nearby streets. The skin was burned off some of them and was hanging from their hands and from their chins."*
(Anon, five-year-old girl)

*"There were a lot of people who were burned to death and among them were some who had burned to a cinder while they were standing up."*
(Anon, four-year-old boy)

**The view from the USA**
*"This is the greatest thing in history."*
(President Harry S Truman)

*"Using atomic bombs against Japan is one of the greatest blunders of history."*
(Leo Szilard, atomic scientist)

What different insights do you get from reading these accounts? Which ones give the most dramatic impression of the event? Are eyewitness records more powerful than second-hand accounts?

# Step 5: Images

Words are the most obvious material in research, but pictures can be almost as important. This is especially true of World War II. For most of history, the only visual records of war had been drawings, paintings, and prints. Most of these were produced days or even years after the event took place.

The earliest wars we can see in photographs are the Crimean War and the American Civil War in the mid-nineteenth century. Movie cameras were used during World War I (1914-1918), recording action sequences for the first time. By the outbreak of World War II, technology had moved on a long way. Film could be shot in colour, and **synchronized sound** could be recorded. The result is a vast and wide-ranging resource of photos, film, and sound.

## Drawings and paintings

Artists still had a part to play in chronicling World War II. Many were employed by governments as official war artists, and painted everything from battle action to horrific scenes from liberated death camps, such as Belsen. Whilst war art is not as minutely accurate or as immediate as photographs, it can still convey impressions and emotions in an individual way.

*This vivid picture of Ruby Loftus, a UK munitions worker, was painted by the war artist Laura Knight.*

Is this quality likely to be useful in a research project? There are certainly many dramatic examples. For instance, anyone whose topic is the home front should look at Henry Moore's drawings of people sheltering in London Underground stations, or at Laura Knight's paintings of women **munitions** workers and **land girls**.

## Photos as hard evidence

Photographs did not just capture significant events in the war. They also provided vital information about the enemy. Aerial pictures, taken from bombers and spy planes, revealed many things such as:

- troop positions and movements
- the location of secret arms factories
- the layout of airfields and military camps
- the extent of damage by bombing raids
- the condition of strategic bridges and tunnels.

In some cases, nobody realized at the time how important some photos were. For example, on 25 August 1944, an RAF aircraft took photographs above the  concentration camp at Auschwitz in Poland. The picture clearly shows the gas chambers and crematoria, and even a train and a line of prisoners. Nobody identified these features until after the war ended.

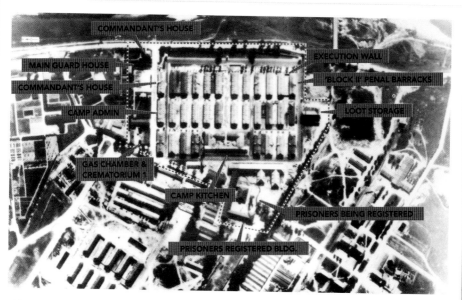

*This aerial view of the Auschwitz concentration camp was taken by an RAF plane in 1944.*

# Moving pictures

By the beginning of World War II, film cameras had become lighter and more efficient than ever before. As a result, film camera operators were able to take footage of almost every aspect of the conflict. There are moving images of everything from the Battle of Britain and the D-Day landings to Japanese *kamikaze* attacks and the liberation of Belsen concentration camp.

Much of this film is easily available, online, in DVDs from shops and libraries, and from museums. The Imperial War Museum in London, for example, has 36 million metres (120 million feet) of cine film and 10,000 hours of video tape.

## War in the cinema

Since 1945, hundreds of cinema films have been made about incidents in World War II. Many of them, such as *The Bridge on the River Kwai* and *Saving Private Ryan*, became box-office smash hits. A huge number are available on DVD, and are frequently screened on television. But do they have any value as research material?

War films can be divided into three main categories:

- Adventure stories: These include thrilling yarns like *The Guns of Navarone* (1961), *Kelly's Heroes* (1970), *The Eagle Has Landed* (1976), and *Saving Private Ryan* (1998). Most of them are fictitious tales, based on real events, and are not very reliable for facts.
- Human drama: These tell personal stories. Some are based on real lives, such as *Das Boot* (1981), *Schindler's List* (1993), *Band of Brothers* (2001), and *The Pianist* (2002). They are usually well researched, and fairly realistically filmed.
- Historical reconstruction: Films such as *A Bridge Too Far* (1977), *Pearl Harbor* (2001), and *Letters From Iwo Jima* (2006) are careful and spectacular re-creations of major events. Some give a fairly faithful picture of what really happened.

## Hollywood and hokum

But beware! All of these cinema films are really fakes. Even the most realistic and true-to-life productions feature actors in make-up, with lots of special effects, stunts, and computer-animated graphics. They are not the real thing, and cannot be used to provide concrete evidence for events which actually happened. Worse still, many films deliberately mislead the viewer. In many cases the real horrors of war are cleaned up or sanitized. The glorious moments are exaggerated for propaganda reasons, while uncomfortable aspects of a story are disguised or omitted. Some films even rewrite history. The most famous recent example of this is *U-571* (2000), in which U.S. sailors board a German submarine and capture an Enigma cipher machine, which helps change the course of the war. In real life, however, the ship and sailors were British.

## Classic images

Many photos and movie clips have become icons of the 20th century. They sum up the pivotal moments and emotional highlights of the war. Some of the most famous include: British troops in the water off Dunkirk, De Gaulle at the Arc de Triomphe after the liberation of Paris, Jews in the Warsaw Ghetto, a sailor kissing a nurse on VJ Day, U.S. troops planting the American flag on Iwo Jima, and Germans soldiers in wintry snow in the Soviet Union.

*This famous photograph shows U.S. troops raising the American flag on the Pacific island of Iwo Jima.*

# How to evaluate images

A careful study of photographs and film stills can sometimes give you a better insight into World War II events and personalities than books and websites. When analyzing an image, concentrate on:

- The details of uniforms, weapons, buildings, and so on. Does the picture match information in documents describing the same subject?
- The way the subject of the picture is represented. How does this affect what you think about the person, place, or event?
- The authenticity of the scene. Do you think it may have been manipulated and details changed? (See page 37.)
- The impact of the image. If you are going to use it in your presentation, is it a clear and vivid picture which will make a dramatic point?

## Can the camera lie?

Just as we have to read documents and books critically, we must also look critically at photographs and documentary film. Sometimes they don't show exactly what they say. For example, news film footage from 1942 apparently shows engineers called **sappers** clearing mines during the Battle of El Alamein in North Africa. In fact, this sequence was filmed later at Pinewood Studios in England.

One of the most famous images of the war shows soldiers hoisting the Soviet flag over the Reichstag in Berlin after fierce fighting in 1945. It was claimed that this happened at 10:50 at night. Yet the scene is in daylight, and there is no sign of fighting. In fact it was probably taken the next day.

These images were created in a different time or place from the real thing, in order to make them look clearer or more dramatic. They were then used for propaganda purposes. They are genuine photographs, but they are misleading and factually incorrect. When you make use of photographs in your research, check carefully that they are an honest record of an actual event.

## Sight and sound

The sounds of the war can have a powerful effect. Looking at film of a Stuka dive bomber is scary enough, but hearing the scream of their sirens as they dive is far scarier. Other famous wartime sounds include air-raid sirens, the thunder of bombers, the thud of bombs exploding, and the tramp of marching feet.

For technical reasons, it was difficult for documentary film-makers during the war to record sound at the same time as filming. As a result there is little film with its own synchronized sound. Most of the films you see will actually have sound added from other sources, such as existing recordings or special sound effects.

## "Doctored" photographs

Photographs can lie in other ways. Today we can easily alter or falsify images by using special computer programs, such as Photoshop. Even without these modern tools, technicians during World War II were able to "doctor" (alter) photos by removing or adding figures, or by changing their positions.

Below is one classic example. In 1942 the Italian dictator Benito Mussolini had his photograph taken in this dramatic horseback pose. To make himself look more heroic, he demanded that the horse handler be removed from the picture.

*This is the original photograph of the Italian leader Benito Mussolini on horseback. The horse handler (outlined in red) was cut from the image before it was shown to the public.*

# Step 6: Other Sources

You can find plenty of fascinating information about World War II outside the library or the computer screen. Many of the effects of the conflict live on – in buildings and other sites, in museums, and in the memories of the participants. These may be slightly more difficult to locate than websites and books, but they will put you more closely in touch with hard reality.

## Witnesses to war

The war ended less than seventy years ago. This means it is still "within living memory". In other words, many people who lived through the conflict are still alive. As adults, they may have served in the armed forces, or worked in factories. As children, they may have been evacuated from their homes or lost loved ones in the fighting.

Do you have any family, neighbours, or relatives of friends who took part in the war, or have first-hand memories of it? If so, ask if they would be willing to answer questions about their experiences. Perhaps they will give you fascinating – and unique – evidence for your project. Act sensitively: they will all be elderly people by now. But remember that some may never have talked about their wartime lives before, and they may find their memories too distressing to discuss.

*Many adults have memories of the war. These British children were evacuated from cities by train to safer areas of the country: now they would be over 70 years old.*

## War of words

Many eyewitness accounts of wartime life have been recorded. These are not widely available, but you should be able to trace some through World War II websites (try national government archive sites) or local libraries. Remember that many other important **oral** records of the war are also preserved on tape and disc. These include great speeches (such as those of Winston Churchill), first-hand reports of events by radio journalists, and talks on the radio by well-known writers, politicians, and other commentators.

## Look around you

Most parts of Europe, as well as many areas in East Asia and the Pacific, suffered bomb and shell damage during the war. Several major cities were almost completely destroyed in the bombing. These included Dresden and Hamburg in Germany, Warsaw in Poland, and of course Hiroshima in Japan. Most have since been rebuilt, some with exact copies of the original old buildings. Hundreds of other towns were badly damaged. If you know where and how to look, you can find evidence of this.

## Finding local evidence

### In towns and cities
The ruins have gone, but it is still possible to spot places where bombs fell. Look for gaps in terraces of pre-war houses or lines of buildings which end abruptly. You may be able to see buildings patched with large areas of different-coloured brick or pockmarks on walls and buildings caused by shrapnel and flying fragments.

### In the countryside
The countryside escaped most of the bombing, but war still left its marks. Look for bomb craters in fields, small block houses or "pillboxes" built for defence in case of invasion, and signs of military training, such as firing ranges or practice trenches.

### At the seaside
In some places, the seaside was the front line. This is especially true of the Channel coasts of the Netherlands, Northern France, and England. Look for concrete defensive works, including bunkers, machine gun posts, and command centres.

There are several websites which will guide you to these wartime remains all over the world (try www.sitesofww2.com).

## The hardware of war

No war before or since has used so much machinery. A vast number of tanks, trucks, guns, aircraft, warships, and radio equipment were produced at high speed. Added to this were millions of shells, bullets, and bombs, as well as personal items, such as uniforms, packs, medals, gas masks, and **ration books**.

Many of these articles survived the war. Some smaller articles may still be treasured as keepsakes by members of your family. There are also many museums which contain important relics from World War II.

## Visiting museums

There's nothing like the real thing. Actually seeing (and maybe handling) objects used in the war can give you direct contact with the physical reality of your topic – something it is hard to get from books and computer screens. Museums offer you the best chance of this contact, but it is vital to choose carefully and make the best use of your time there:

- Establish that the museum has exhibits relevant to your topic.
- Make sure of the museum's opening hours and location.
- Buy a museum guide: it will help you find what you're looking for, and may have useful information on your subject area. You may also be able to use it as part of your presentation.
- Spend time looking closely at what you've come to see: think about its size and weight, and imagine carrying it, travelling in it, or using it.
- Read the labels and explanatory panels.
- Make notes or sketches and (if allowed) take photographs.
- Buy postcards from the shop to remind you of your visit, and to use as illustrations for your presentation.

## Memorials of the dead

A memorial is a monument or some other structure which reminds us of a person or event. It can be a simple plaque on a wall or a grand symbol of national grief, such as the Cenotaph in London or Victory Park in Moscow. These places are usually the site for annual ceremonies honouring veterans and victims of the war. They are useful to visit for atmosphere rather than concrete information.

Many towns or villages in countries that took part in the war have war memorials and graveyards, where local soldiers are buried. There are also larger regional and national World War II cemeteries and memorials all over the world. These are very solemn and moving places, but they can also offer fascinating evidence about individual servicemen and women who died in the fighting. You can gather dates, ages, locations, and other details from gravestones and burial records.

## Atmospheric places

Some sites have a very special place in wartime history. Even in such a bloody global conflict, these were the settings for events that were particularly horrific or significant. Visiting these places will give you something that no other research offers – atmosphere. Write down what you feel, as well as what you see. Of course, many people will not be able to make such trips. But if you are ever in a place connected with the war, take time to reflect on the feelings it evokes. Here are a few such places:

*Auschwitz-Birkenau (near Krakow, Poland)*
This was the most infamous of the Nazi death camps, where over a million Jews were killed. You can walk round the vast site, including the railway ramp where the prisoners arrived, the huts where they lived, and the gas chambers where they died. There is also an information centre.

*Oradour-sur-Glane (Limoges, France)*
In June 1944, Nazi soldiers massacred almost every man, woman, and child in this remote French village. They gave no reason. Today Oradour is a monument to the atrocity. The burned and shattered village has been left exactly as it was for visitors to see.

*Hiroshima (Honshu, Japan)*
The atomic bomb killed at least 80,000 instantly, and thousands more in the years since. In the rebuilt city, you can visit the Peace Memorial Park, where the bomb fell, and the Peace Memorial Museum, with exhibits that show the appalling effects of the blast.

*Changi (Singapore)*
Many soldiers and civilians, including children, were held at this Japanese prisoner of war camp for years in terrible conditions. Many died. There is a chapel and museum with personal effects of those who were held at Changi and also those who died during the occupation of Singapore.

*Images like this one of starving prisoners in a Japanese prisoner of war camp can give some idea of the suffering of those who were captured.*

# Step 7: Putting It All Together

By now, you should have assembled the research evidence for your World War II topic. It may be in various forms – handwritten notes, printed sheets, saved computer documents, action photographs, diagrams, lists of casualty statistics, quotations from leaders, and many other things. Your next task is to draw all this together into a clear and well-organized form, ready to submit to your teacher or to present in class.

## Keep focused

At this stage, it is crucial to stay focused on the topic. Remind yourself of exactly what you were setting out to achieve in the beginning. What was the purpose of your research? Look again at the title of your project. Have you fully understood what was wanted and explored every angle? If it was a question, have you answered that question? And are you really satisfied with the answer? Then take a step further. You are going to use your research to answer a specific question. Can it also be used to ask more questions?

Say, for instance, your topic is "What were the causes of World War II?" You've gathered plenty of evidence about the economic slump, the rise of fascism, and the growth of nationalist ambitions. But you feel there is more. Was the outbreak of the war entirely due to German aggression? Was the weak response of Britain and France partly to blame? What about the attitude of the Soviet Union? And so on. Tackling these questions will add an extra dimension to your work.

### Get yourself organized

Locating, reading, evaluating, and noting information can be a complicated process. When you've done it several times with different sources, it can seem like a maze of facts and figures. If you were well organized from the start, you'll find this becomes even more important as you approach the climax of your project. Here are some tips to help you:

- Have a work station, so you can do all your organizing of research materials in one place.
- Try to keep a clean, uncluttered surface to work on – as big as possible.
- Give yourself plenty of time: set aside a regular, fixed period for working and keep to it.

- Create your own system for arranging your material in an orderly way: put things in neat piles, boxes, or files – whatever suits you best.
- Don't get distracted: turn off the TV and avoid the temptation to surf the net for material not related to the topic.
- Tidy up your work station when you finish your session: it will be easier to start work again next time.

## A pie chart

A pie chart is a simple and effective way of showing how different-sized parts of a total relate to the whole. Why a pie? Because it looks like a pie from above – each part becomes a slice of the whole. The chart is a circle, which represents the total. Each slice, or segment, represents a part. Here is an example of how a pie chart can present information:

### What kinds of people were killed in the Holocaust?

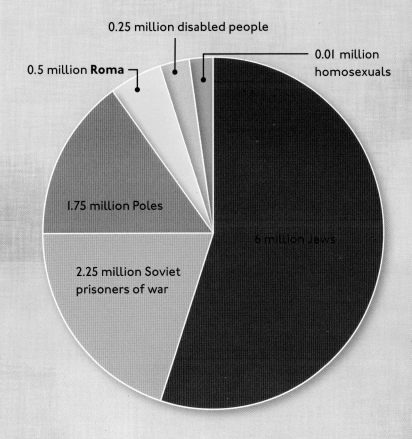

0.25 million disabled people

0.5 million **Roma**

0.01 million homosexuals

1.75 million Poles

2.25 million Soviet prisoners of war

6 million Jews

## Answering a question

Suppose someone asks you "What year did World War II begin?" It is a simple question and it has one correct answer: 1939. If you replied "1938" or "1940" you would be wrong. The war's starting date is a fact which nobody can dispute.

The title of your project may well ask a question, too, but it won't be as simple as that. It could be "Why did the Holocaust happen?", or "Was Hitler's invasion of the Soviet Union a mistake?", or "What was life like in London during the Blitz?". There are no correct or definite answers to any of these questions.

All the same, you need to come up with an answer. This will be based on what you find during your research work, which will help you to form an opinion. You may start off with a fixed idea of your answer, but as you learn more about the topic this may change. Be open minded.

44

### Right you ARE: How to present an argument

If you put forward an opinion, you must be able to support it. Remember these three steps, called A-R-E.
Assertion: You state your opinion.
Reasoning: You give the reasons why you formed your opinion.
Evidence: You use facts to back up your opinion and show it is valid.

### Looking at both sides of a question

Do you already know something about the topic you are researching? Do you already think you have an answer to the question? Think again. It is a mistake to start out with a fixed opinion in your head and then try to justify it. Keep an open mind at the beginning, and don't ignore evidence and views just because you disagree with them.

If you don't have an opinion to begin with, you should be trying to form one. As you proceed with your work, you are likely to find facts and interpretations which conflict with each other. Remember that there are at least two answers to every question. In most cases, there is some value in these differing points of view.

For example, your topic is "Were the Allies justified in dropping atomic bombs on Japan?" One source tells you they were justified (the bombs brought a swift Japanese surrender, thus avoiding many months of extra bloodshed). Another source believes the bombing was not justified (the scale of the destruction was so horrific that no civilized country should have caused it). You have to look at both sides of the argument and weigh up the evidence. Certainly you should include both opinions in your written presentation.

## Using a Venn diagram

This is another type of graphic organizer. You can use it to compare and contrast information, and to illustrate common points and differences. A Venn diagram consists of two or more circles which overlap, representing different subjects. In the large areas of each circle, you list the unique aspects of each subject. In the central overlap, you list things they have in common. This Venn diagram compares some of the aims and beliefs of Germany and the Soviet Union at the time of their Pact of 1939.

**Germany**

Right-wing fascism

Persecution of ethnic minority groups

Encouragement of free enterprise

Hitler's hatred of Slav peoples

Rule by dictator as one-party state

Repressive (harsh) laws against opponents

Desire to regain territory lost after World War I

Desire to force their own beliefs on the rest of the world

**Soviet Union**

Left-wing communism

State ownership of all property, land, and the means of producing goods

Belief that war would weaken capitalist nations of the west

## How to approach a topic

Here is a specimen topic, with some guidance ideas. It suggests ways to approach the subject, and possible sources to use for research. It also provides a list of avenues to explore – extra questions which may crop up as you pursue your inquiries. The topic question is: **How decisive was the U.S. entry into World War II?**

## About the question

First of all, ask yourself the 5 Ws – Who? What? When? Where? Why? Write down your findings to create a basic framework for the subject.

Then think about how much the question involves. What, in simple terms, is the background to this topic? At the outbreak of war, the USA stayed neutral. Then came the Japanese attack on Pearl Harbor, and soon the Americans were fighting alongside Allied troops. They played a major role in many areas of the war, notably the Pacific conflict and the liberation of Europe.

## Create a timeline relevant to the question

| 1939 | September | President Roosevelt announces U.S. neutrality |
|------|-----------|-----------------------------------------------|
| **1941** | March | Congress approves Lend-Lease Act, giving financial aid to Allied countries |
| | December | Japanese aircraft attack U.S. Pacific fleet in Pearl Harbor, Hawaii; USA declares war on Japan; Germany declares war on USA |
| **1942** | February | **Internment** of 120,000 Japanese Americans and Japanese nationals in USA begins |
| | June | U.S. fleet defeats Japanese at Battle of Midway |
| **1943** | September | U.S. troops take part in Allied invasion of mainland Italy |
| **1944** | June | U.S. troops take part in Allied landings in France |
| | October | U.S. troops land in the Philippines |
| **1945** | March | U.S. marines capture Iwo Jima |
| | August | U.S. plane drops atomic bomb on Hiroshima |

## Sources to look at

- A website: www.pbs.org/perilousfight
  This PBS website offers a great overview of World War II, including a timeline.
- A book: *The United States and World War II: The Awakening Giant* by Martin Folly (Edinburgh University Press, 2002).
- Primary sources: *War As I Knew It* by George S. Patton (Houghton Mifflin 1995). Vivid battle accounts by the brilliant and controversial U.S. general.

- Archives: www.archives.gov/research/ww2/.
  Vast selection of records from the National
  Archives of the USA.

## Places to visit
In Europe:
- D-Day Museum, Museum Road, Portsmouth, UK
- Museum of the Battle of Normandy, Boulevard Fabian Ware,
  Bayeux, France
- Auschwitz-Birkenau Concentration Camp historical site and museum,
  near Krakow, Poland

In the USA:
- National World War II Museum, 945 Magazine Street, New Orleans,
  Louisiana, USA

## Quotes
*"Yesterday, December seventh, 1941, a date which will live in infamy, the
United States of America was suddenly and deliberately attacked by naval
and air forces of the Empire of Japan."* President Franklin D. Roosevelt

*"Now it is impossible for us to lose the war."* Adolf Hitler, on hearing of the
Japanese attack on Pearl Harbor

*"We are no longer alone."* Winston Churchill, after the bombing of
Pearl Harbor

## Some other questions to think about
Here are some extra questions which you might want to include in
your research:
- If the USA had declared war on Germany in 1939, would Hitler have acted
  differently? Would his fear of American military strength have made him
  change his invasion plans?
- Why did Roosevelt help Britain by providing arms through the Lend-Lease
  Act when his country was still officially neutral?
- Even if Pearl Harbor never happened, would the United States have
  entered the war at some stage?
- If the USA had remained out of the conflict altogether, would the Allies
  still have won?
- Did the wealth and industrial strength of the USA allow it to develop
  better technology – aircraft, guns, bombs, communications – than other
  nations? And why did Hitler ignore this?
- What advantages did the USA gain from helping to defeat the
  Axis powers?

# Step 8: Presentation

You've completed your research, organized your findings, and checked that the important questions have been answered. Now comes the final step: writing it all down. This is often the most daunting part of the project, because you have to communicate what you have learned to other people.

This presentation may be a written document, with illustrations and other visual aids, for your teacher or assessor. Maybe it is an oral presentation which you make to fellow students. In both cases, you must have a clear **thesis** (argument), with plenty of evidence to back it up – the more dramatic the better.

## Writing it down: a simple guide

1. Make a rough outline of your thesis, broken down into paragraphs for the different parts. This should have an introduction, a main section with evidence, and a conclusion.
2. Work out your word count. What is the total of words required? Divide this up fairly equally between the sections, and write in these sub-totals on the outline.
3. Get writing! Stick to your outline plan and go through section by section. Try to keep to the word totals: extra writing is a waste of time.
4. Explain things as clearly as possible. Avoid long words and pompous phrases. Keep your sentences mostly short and simple.
5. Be selective. Weed out anything which is irrelevant or just a repetition of a previous statement.
6. Write at a good speed without rushing. Don't worry about making mistakes at this stage – you can always correct them later.

### Footnotes and endnotes

Sometimes, you may wish to provide extra pieces of important information which don't fit comfortably into the main text. You can add these either as footnotes (at the foot of the page), or as endnotes (at the end of the text). Several computer programs will help you to create or manage these. There are two kinds of notes. The first gives another fact or explanation relating to something in the main text. These are known as annotated footnotes or endnotes. The second kind of note simply lists the source of the information used or directly quoted, giving full details of the author, publisher, publication date, and the relevant page number.

## The bibliography

A bibliography is a list of the most important books and other sources used in your research project. The sources are usually arranged at the end of the work, in alphabetical order by the authors' surnames. The list should include all the sources you have quoted or taken material from. Each entry in a bibliography states the author, title, publisher, and date of publication. Sometimes the place of publication is given, too.

There are several ways to create a bibliography. Talk to your teacher about what is required. Here are some basic rules for setting out your sources:

*Book*
Author's last name, author's first name (or initials). Book title. Place of publication: publisher, publication date – for example: Rhodes, Richard. *The Making of the Atomic Bomb*. London: Simon & Schuster, 1986

*Magazine/journal/periodical*
Author's last name, author's first name (or initials). "Title of article." Title of magazine/newspaper. Volume, date: page number(s) – for example: Hauner, Milan. "Did Hitler Want a World Dominion?" *Journal of Contemporary History*. Vol. 13, No. 1, Jan 1978: 15-32

*Encyclopedia*
Author (if known). "Title of article." Encyclopedia title. Volume, date – for example: Stokesbury, James L. "World War Two." *World Book*. Vol 21, 2007

*Website*
Author (if known). "Title of article." Title of web page. Publisher. Publication date. Web address – for example: Various authors. "*Short Essays*." Holocaust History Project. January 2006. www.holocaust-history.org/short-essays/

## Written presentation checklist

- Have you stated your thesis clearly and concisely at the beginning?
- Did you follow your outline? Or did you miss things out?
- Are your points made in a logical sequence?
- Have you given proper references for your sources?
- Is everything (apart from acknowledged quotations) written in your own words?
- Have you made any mistakes in grammar, word use, or spelling? Use a dictionary or thesaurus if necessary, and run a spell check on your computer.
- Have you asked someone else to read it over? He or she might spot mistakes you missed.

## How to make an oral presentation

Standing up in front of your classmates to read your own work can be a nerve-racking experience. But if you prepare thoroughly and follow a few simple tips, it will be a lot easier. Set aside a period of time well beforehand for getting ready.

Practise reading some passages from your project out loud. How does it sound? Jot down in the margin reminders of anything extra you want to say. Remember that you should begin by stating your subject and giving a simple description of what you are about to examine. You can also explain why you chose this topic, and the most important things you learned during your research.

## Oral presentation checklist

- Speak clearly in your normal voice, and loudly enough for everyone to hear.
- Stand up straight and don't move about too much.
- Look up and make eye contact with your listeners.
- Vary the pitch and volume of your voice.
- Leave time at the end for people to ask questions.

Print out and collect together the pictures and diagrams you want to use during your talk. Are they going to be large enough for everyone to see? Think of other objects you can show to illustrate the topic. If you are using electronic aids, such as DVDs, CDs, digital projectors, or computers, make sure they are correctly set up.

## Remember the eight steps to use in researching a topic

### Step 1: The overview

Look at a broad outline of World War II and its main events. Once you have a basic knowledge of the causes of the conflict and its course, you will be in a better position to select a topic for your own special project.

### Step 2: The basics

Find out about the different research tools and how to access them. The Internet and books are the most obvious ones, but you should learn how to use them effectively. Graphic organizers are also valuable tools for arranging information.

### Step 3: Digging deeper

It's time to decide on your special topic. If possible, choose an aspect of World War II which interests you. If a subject seems too big, narrow it down to make it more manageable. If it seems too small, then broaden it out to provide more context.

## Step 4: Documents

Documents are the raw material of history, usually written at the time by people who were directly involved with events. Documents come in many forms, including diaries, letters, poems, government reports, military records, and newspaper articles.

## Step 5: Images

Pictures can have just as much impact as words. World War II was the first to be recorded in huge detail in photographs and movie film. But images, just like documents, can be misleading and must be looked at critically.

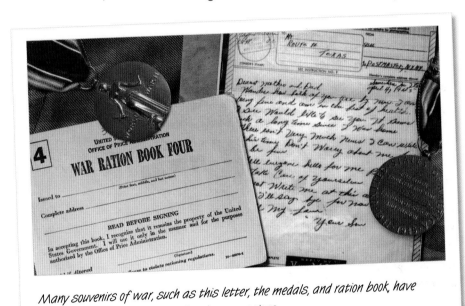

*Many souvenirs of war, such as this letter, the medals, and ration book, have survived in museums and as family possessions.*

## Step 6: Other sources

You can find plenty of fascinating information about the war away from libraries or computers. Crucial evidence lives on in the memories of those who took part, as well as in monuments, cemeteries, damaged buildings, and museums.

## Step 7: Putting it all together

Your next task is to assemble your evidence – notes, printed sheets, images and quotations – into a clear and well-organized form. Keep focused on the topic, and remind yourself of exactly what questions you were setting out to answer.

## Step 8: The presentation

This is perhaps the hardest part – writing your assignment in its final form and (maybe) presenting it in front of a class. Create an outline and stick to it, then carefully check through your finished text.

# Glossary

**Anderson shelter**  bomb shelter made of corrugated metal, named after a British politician

**appeasement**  giving concessions to possible enemies with the aim of keeping peace

**archives**  place where records and other documents are kept

**atomic bomb**  (see nuclear bomb)

**blitzkrieg**  form of all-out and rapid attack, from the German words *blitz* (lightning) and *krieg* (war)

**blog**  short for "web log": a public Internet diary or newsletter kept by someone online

**chronology**  list of events or dates in their correct calendar sequence

**cipher**  system of secret writing in which letters are rearranged or replaced

**code breaker**  person who works out the operation of an enemy cipher or code, allowing his or her side to read enemy messages

**communism**  social and political system in which property and the means of production are owned by the people of a country

**concentration camp**  compound where enemy soldiers or civilians are imprisoned. It is generally used to describe camps where Nazis held Jews and other persecuted people.

**D-Day**  official name for the day on which the Allied invasion of Europe began during World War II (6 June 1944)

**democracy**  system of government in which the people of a country elect their own rulers

**depression**  period when economic conditions decline drastically, with falling prices and rising unemployment

**dictator**  ruler who has complete control over a country and its people

**Enigma**  German machine which turned an ordinary message into cipher text

**expansionism**  policy of increasing the size or areas under the control of a country by expanding into neighbouring territory

**fascism**  system of government where control is in the hands of extreme right-wing rulers

**"Final Solution"**  Nazi plan for the mass killing of European Jews

**firestorm**  violent storm caused by hot air rising from an area that is on fire. The resulting very high winds make the fires burn more fiercely.

**ghetto**  section of a city where Jews or other minority groups are confined

**internment**  in this context, forced confinement in U.S. camps of Japanese Americans and Japanese nationals from February 1942. Up to 120,000 were held in these camps. Those held were released from January 1945.

**Iron Curtain**  imaginary line, which divided the communist states of Eastern Europe from Western Europe during the Cold War

**kamikaze**  Japanese pilot trained to fly an aircraft in a suicide crash attack

**land girls**  female farm workers who took the place of men serving in the armed forces

**liberate**  to free or release an area of territory from oppressive enemy rule

**memoirs**  person's memories set down in book form

**microfiche**  sheet of microfilm capable of carrying a huge number of pages of information in reduced form

**morale**  state of mind (such as level of happiness or unhappiness) of a person or group

**munitions**  materials produced for war, such as weapons and ammunition

**neutral**  not joining either side in a war or dispute

**newsreel**  short film which presents news items

**nuclear bomb**  explosive weapon of great power released by splitting the nuclei (the central parts of atoms) of certain radioactive materials, such as uranium

**oral**  spoken (rather than written)

**plagiarism**  stealing another person's writings or thoughts and presenting them as your own

**primary source**  material about an event which comes from someone or something present at the time

**propaganda**  promoting or discrediting of an idea or belief using biased materials, such as speeches or posters or leaflets

**radar**  method of detecting distant objects by bouncing radio waves off them

**ration book**  book of coupons which allows someone to buy a fixed amount of goods during a time of national shortages

**refugee**  person forced to flee their home due to war, natural disaster, or other violent event

**Roma**  travelling people who speak the Romany language. They are also known as "gypsies".

**sapper**  soldier who works as an engineer in tasks such as building bridges and clearing minefields

**secondary source**  material about an event which is produced by someone after the event, usually using primary sources

**Soviet Union (USSR)**  federation (group) of communist states which dominated Eastern Europe and North Asia from 1922 until its break up in 1991

**synchronized sound**  sound track which operates in unison with moving film images. Synchronized sound is usually recorded at the same time as the filming.

**theatre of war**  one of the regions where major episodes of a conflict take place

**thesis**  subject of a report or essay, or argument made in them

**Third Reich**  government established in Germany by Adolf Hitler in 1933

**totalitarian**  kind of government in which total control of the population is achieved by repressive means

**treaty**  formal agreement between two or more states concerning peace, trade, or an alliance

# Find Out More

## Books and websites

Thousands of books have been written about all aspects of World War II, and millions of Internet websites are devoted to it. This is just a tiny selection. Look in your library catalogue by typing in "World War II", and add your special subject, or browse online.

### General accounts

Connolly, Sean. *Witness to History: World War II.* Oxford: Heinemann Library, 2004.

Keegan, John. *World War Two in Photographs.* The Imperial War Museum. London: Carlton Books, 2000.

Mercer, Derrick, ed. *Chronicle of the Second World War.* London: Longman, 1990.

Wint, Guy, Peter Calvocoressi, and John Pritchard. *The Penguin History of the Second World War.* London: Penguin, 1999.

www.bbc.co.uk/history/worldwars/wwtwo

www.secondworldwar.co.uk/

www.spartacus.schoolnet.co.uk/2WWchron.htm
A very useful timeline of World War II

### The Home Front

Arthur, Max. *Forgotten Voices of the Second World War: A New History of the Second World War and the Men and Women Who Were There.* London: Ebury Press, 2005.

Wing, Sandra Koa, ed. *Our Longest Days: A People's History of the Second World War by the Writers of Mass Observation.* London: Profile, 2008.

www.nationalarchives.gov.uk/catalogue/RdLeaflet.asp?sLeafletID=241
Has a special section on the Home Front.

www.war-experience.org

## The Holocaust

Gilbert, Martin. *The Holocaust: A History of the Jews of Europe During the Second World War.* London: Henry Holt, 1986.

Shuter, Jane. *The Holocaust: Life and Death in Hitler's Europe.* Oxford: Heinemann Library, 2004.

Smith, Lyn. *Forgotten Voices of the Holocaust: A New History in the Words of the Men and Women Who Survived.* London: Ebury Press, 2006.

Willoughby, Susan. *20th Century Perspectives: The Holocaust.* Oxford: Heinemann Library, 2001.

www.holocaust-history.org

www.holocaustsurvivors.org

www.auschwitz.org.pl

## The Atomic Bomb

Harris, Nathaniel. *Witness to History: Hiroshima.* Oxford: Heinemann Library, 2004.

Hersey, John. *Hiroshima.* London: Penguin, 1946.

Rhodes, Richard. *The Making of the Atomic Bomb.* London: Simon & Schuster, 1986.

Tames, Richard. *Turning Points in History: Hiroshima, Shadow of the Bomb.* Oxford: Heinemann Library, 2006.

www.pcf.city.hiroshima.jp/index_e2.html

www.gwu.edu/~nsarchiv/NSAEBB/NSAEBB162/index.htm
  U.S. government archive covering the building of the bomb

## The Secret War

Sebag-Montefiroe, Hugh. *Enigma: The Battle for the Code.* London: Phoenix, 2001.

Weitz, Margaret Collins. *Sisters in the Resistance: How Women Fought to Free France, 1940-45.* London: Wiley, 1998.

www.bletchleypark.org.uk/
  The home of Allied secret intelligence, where the Enigma cipher was cracked.

www.historylearningsite.co.uk/resistance_movements.htm

# Index